SPORTS ALL-STARS

AARON RODGERS

Jon M. Fishman

Lerner Publications ◆ Minneapolis

Lerner Publications Company
A division of Lerner Publishing Group, Inc.
241 First Avenue North
Minneapolis, MN 55401 USA

For reading levels and more information, look up this title at www.lernerbooks.com.

Main body text set in Albany Std 15/22. Typeface provided by Agfa.

Library of Congress Cataloging-in-Publication Data

Names: Fishman, Jon M., author.
Title: Aaron Rodgers / Jon M. Fishman.
Description: Minneapolis : Lerner Publications, [2019] | Series: Sports All-Stars |
    Includes bibliographical references and index. | Audience: Ages: 7–11. | Audience:
    Grades: 4 to 6.
Identifiers: LCCN 2017049356 (print) | LCCN 2017052087 (ebook) |
    ISBN 9781541524613 (eb pdf) | ISBN 9781541524538 (library binding : alk.
    paper) | ISBN 9781541527997 (paperback : alk. paper)
Subjects: LCSH: Rodgers, Aaron, 1983—Juvenile literature. | Football players—
    United States—Biography—Juvenile literature. | Quarterbacks (Football)—United
    States—Biography—Juvenile literature.
Classification: LCC GV939.R6235 (ebook) | LCC GV939.R6235 F57 2019 (print) |
    DDC 796.332092 [B]—dc23

LC record available at https://lccn.loc.gov/2017049356

Manufactured in the United States of America
1-44529-34779-4/5/2018

CONTENTS

300 4

California Quarterback 8

Packing on Muscle 13

Fame and Fortune 18

Super Packer 24

All-Star Stats 28

Source Notes 29

Glossary 30

Further Information 31

Index 32

Aaron Rodgers passes the ball on September 17, 2017.

Aaron Rodgers and the Green Bay Packers were getting crushed. They trailed the Atlanta Falcons by 24 points on September 17, 2017. It was only the second game of the National Football League (NFL) season for Green Bay. The Packers had plenty of games left to improve, but Rodgers wasn't ready to give up against Atlanta.

Rodgers stepped back to pass. He turned to his left and launched the ball. It soared to **wide receiver** Davante Adams. Adams snagged the ball just as he fell into the end zone. The 33-yard pass was the 299th touchdown throw of Rodgers's career.

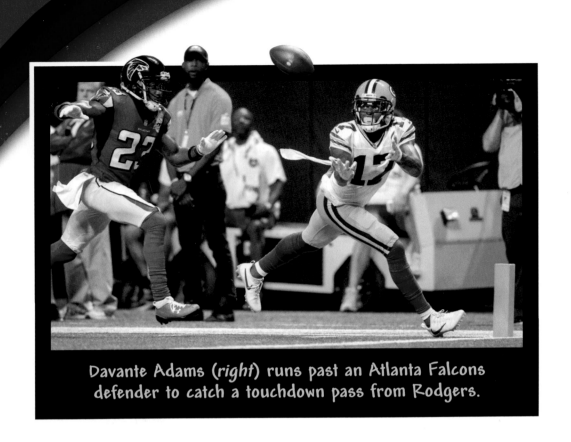

Davante Adams (*right*) runs past an Atlanta Falcons defender to catch a touchdown pass from Rodgers.

When Rodgers joined the Packers in 2005, the team already had a star quarterback. Brett Favre played for Green Bay for 16 seasons. In 1997, he led the team to victory in Super Bowl XXXI. He set many NFL records by the time he retired from football. Rodgers mostly sat on the bench for three years, watching Favre play.

Favre left Green Bay in 2008. Rodgers wasted no time proving that the Packers still had a superstar quarterback. His running and throwing power wowed fans. Even more impressive was his accuracy. Through 2016, Rodgers averaged fewer than eight **interceptions** a season. He has the lowest rate of interceptions of any quarterback in NFL history.

Against the Falcons, Rodgers drove the Packers to Atlanta's 1-yard line. He flipped the ball to teammate Ty Montgomery, who dashed in for a touchdown and Rodgers's 300th passing score.

The touchdown made the final score Atlanta 34, Green Bay 23. Rodgers had reached 300 touchdowns in fewer games than any quarterback in NFL history. It was just the latest record-setting moment in Rodgers's incredible career.

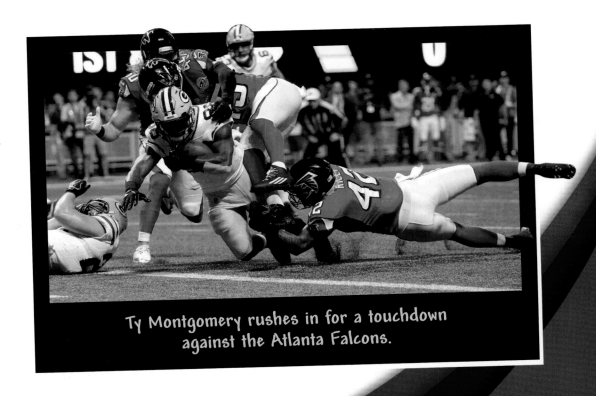

Ty Montgomery rushes in for a touchdown against the Atlanta Falcons.

CALIFORNIA
QUARTERBACK

Rodgers plays in a college football game in 2003.

Aaron Rodgers was born on December 2, 1983, in Chico, California. He grew up there with his parents and two brothers.

Sports fans in California are wild about

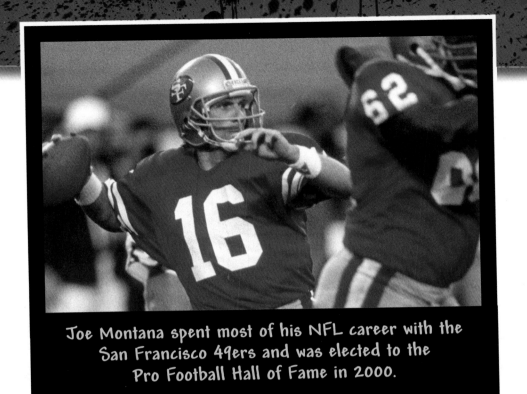

Joe Montana spent most of his NFL career with the San Francisco 49ers and was elected to the Pro Football Hall of Fame in 2000.

football. Many NFL players came from the state—especially quarterbacks. Aaron learned about the sport from his dad. Ed Rodgers had played college football at California State University, Chico.

By the time he was two years old, Aaron enjoyed watching NFL games on TV. He would watch the whole game and barely take his eyes off the screen. He especially liked watching the San Francisco 49ers. He would try to guess the play that Joe Montana, San Francisco's quarterback, was going to run next.

Football wasn't the only sport that Aaron liked. He played soccer, basketball, and baseball too. He often wanted to be the star of the team. "I was always drawn to being in positions where I had an impact on the game," he said. He played **point guard** on the basketball court. He enjoyed playing goalie during soccer games and pitcher for the baseball team.

Other sports were fun for him, but clearly, Aaron had a special talent for football. Friends say he could throw with amazing strength at the age of five— and he could hit his target. He later threw a football over his friends' three-story house and into their pool in the backyard.

Being tall helps a quarterback see open wide receivers. Aaron had a strong arm, but he wasn't tall. He stood

Aaron played quarterback for Pleasant Valley High School.

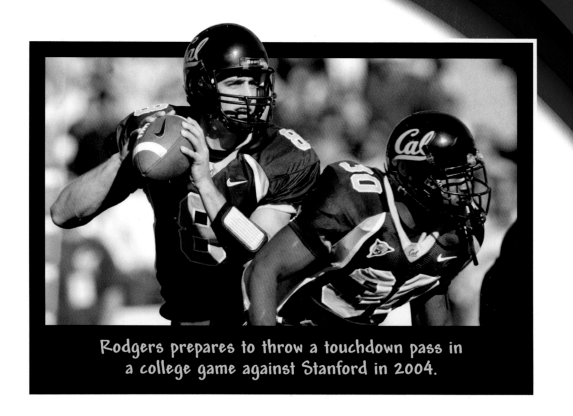

Rodgers prepares to throw a touchdown pass in a college game against Stanford in 2004.

5 feet 3 (1.6 m) as a high school freshman. He shot up to 6 feet (1.8 m) by his senior season. He had grown a lot in three years, but he was still shorter than many college quarterbacks.

Rodgers didn't receive any college **scholarship** offers from schools with top football teams. So he went to Butte College in Oroville, California, in 2002. The school is a **community college**. Rodgers led the Butte Roadrunners to a 10–1 record and the **conference** championship.

Rodgers left Butte after one season to attend the University of California, Berkeley (Cal). His new school

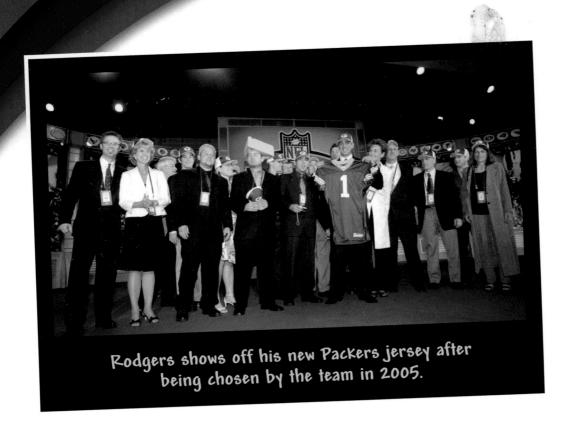

Rodgers shows off his new Packers jersey after being chosen by the team in 2005.

played against tougher competition. But Rodgers proved he could handle it with 19 touchdowns in his first season. Then he threw 24 touchdowns the next year.

In 2005, Rodgers left Cal to join the NFL. Team after team passed on him at the **NFL Draft** that year. But finally, the Packers chose Rodgers with the 24th overall pick. He knew he could be a star in the league. He just needed a chance to play.

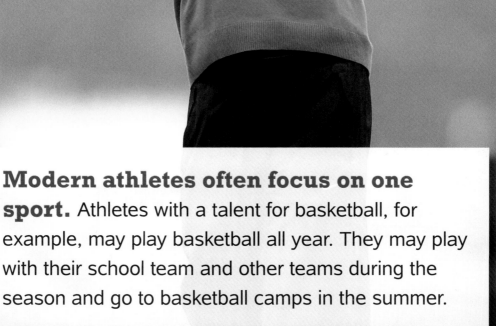

Rodgers enjoys playing many sports, including golf.

Modern athletes often focus on one sport. Athletes with a talent for basketball, for example, may play basketball all year. They may play with their school team and other teams during the season and go to basketball camps in the summer.

Rodgers warms up with his team during a training session in 2017.

Rodgers thinks this is a mistake. He played many sports as a kid, and he believes that helped him become a great quarterback. Different sports have different challenges. Overcoming those challenges can teach kids lessons about sports and life.

Sports also teach skills that athletes can apply to other pursuits. Rodgers often wriggles out of danger and finds open wide receivers on the run. Throwing while running is a skill that he sharpened while playing basketball.

In 2017, Rodgers told a reporter for *Sports Illustrated* that he wanted to play football for up to 10 more years. So he would still be playing at the age of 43. Tom Brady of the New England Patriots is the oldest quarterback in the NFL. He turned 40 in August 2017. Rodgers knows he'll have to work hard to stay fit as he ages, but he's

Rodgers eats mostly vegetables. He rarely has meat and avoids dairy foods. He makes sure about 80 percent of the food he eats is healthful. He has at least one weakness, though: Girl Scout cookies.

Rodgers practices throwing before a game.

ready for the challenge. The older he gets, the more he enjoys workouts and practices. "And when you're loving those things, the game is really icing on the cake for you," Rodgers said.

He spends a lot of time in the gym. Rodgers lifts heavy weights to strengthen the muscles in his stomach and back. These core muscles help athletes stay balanced and steady on their feet. Rodgers also lifts weights to maintain the strength in his legs and throwing arm.

Healthy muscles aren't just strong. They are **flexible** too. Rodgers stretches his muscles often. This helps him move smoothly and easily and avoid injury. **Yoga** is a favorite activity. It does three things at once: it strengthens his muscles, helps them stay flexible, and calms his mind. "Yoga is just wonderful for me," Rodgers said in 2017. "I feel like I am moving as well as I did when I was 23."

Rodgers stretches during a training session in 2017.

FAME AND FORTUNE

Rodgers celebrates
the Green Bay
Packers' win during
Super Bowl XLV.

Rodgers accepts the MVP trophy after his performance in Super Bowl XLV.

The NFL is the most popular sports league in the United States. Becoming an NFL quarterback means instant fame, so Rodgers was already well known when he led the Packers to Super Bowl XLV in 2011. Then he threw three touchdown passes and won the game's Most Valuable Player (MVP) award. Green Bay beat the Pittsburgh Steelers, 31–25, and Rodgers became a sports megastar.

Since then, Rodgers has been on all kinds of TV shows. He played a judge in a singing contest on *The Office*. He's a frequent guest on talk shows such as *The Tonight Show Starring Jimmy Fallon*. In 2017, he was a celebrity contestant on *The $100,000 Pyramid* game show. He was so good at the game that he helped a woman win the $100,000 grand prize!

Jordan Rodgers got engaged to Jojo Fletcher after winning season 12 of *The Bachelorette*.

The spotlight that always shines on NFL quarterbacks has drawbacks too. People said Rodgers had a troubled relationship with his family. His brother Jordan Rodgers confirmed the rumors during an appearance on the TV show *The Bachelorette*.

Some people said the tension came from Aaron Rodgers's fame. Others said his famous girlfriend, actor Olivia Munn, was to blame. Rodgers didn't want to talk about his family. "I think there should be a separation between your public life and your personal life," he said. Rodgers and Munn broke up in 2017.

Rodgers signed a new contract with the Packers in 2013. The team agreed to pay him $110 million over the next five years. That made Rodgers the NFL's top-paid player at the time.

Rodgers and Olivia Munn attended the Academy Awards together in 2016.

Rodgers wears shoes that promote awareness
of childhood cancer.

He uses some of that money to give back to his community. He has helped raise millions of dollars for the Midwest Athletes Against Childhood Cancer Fund. The group helps fight cancer around the world. In 2016, Rodgers wore special shoes during a game to raise awareness for the fund. He also takes part in many other events for charity.

The Quarterback and the President

Before a game in 2015, the Green Bay Packers and the Detroit Lions held a moment of silence to honor victims of a recent terrorist attack in Paris, France. During the moment, a fan yelled an anti-Islamic comment. Rodgers spoke out against the fan's actions after the game.

President Barack Obama heard Rodgers's comments and sent the quarterback a handwritten letter of support. That was just the start of the connection between the two men. Around that time, Obama compared himself to Rodgers in an interview with *GQ* magazine. The president said they both stayed calm under pressure. In 2016, Rodgers even got to golf with Obama. The quarterback said he was nervous at first. But, as usual, he quickly calmed down and played well.

Rodgers presents a jersey to Barack Obama after the Green Bay win in Super Bowl XLV.

SUPER PACKER

Rodgers looks to pass during the 2010 Pro Bowl.

Rodgers has a big contract and a celebrity lifestyle because of his results on the field. Players, coaches, and fans have voted Rodgers to the **Pro Bowl** six times. He won the NFL MVP award in 2011 and 2014.

Green Bay fans celebrate with Rodgers after he scores a touchdown.

More impressive than his personal stats is the way Rodgers makes Green Bay a better team. The Packers had six wins and 10 losses in 2008, his first season as the starting quarterback. Since then, Rodgers has led Green Bay to a winning record nearly every year. He cemented his status as a Packers legend when he became the MVP of Super Bowl XLV.

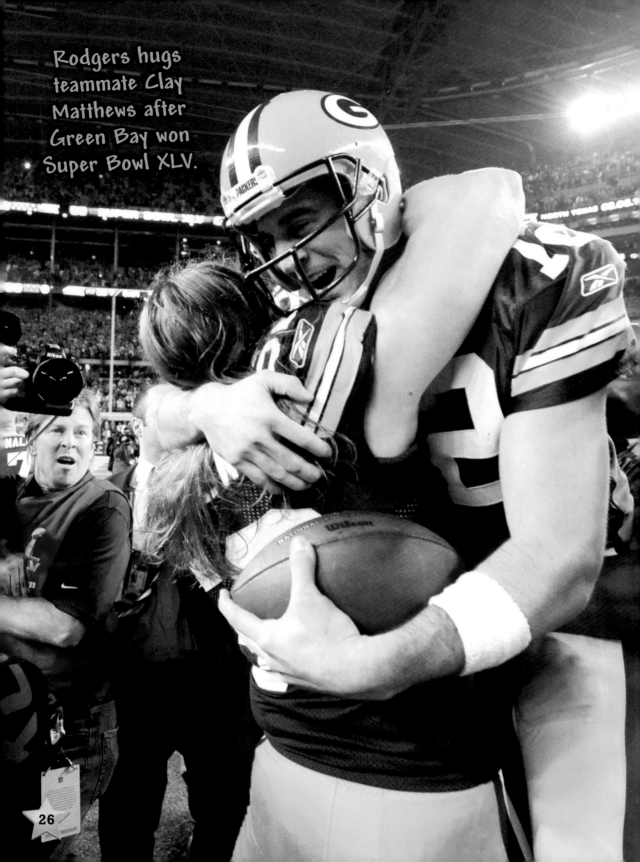

Rodgers hugs teammate Clay Matthews after Green Bay won Super Bowl XLV.

Winning the Super Bowl is the ultimate target for every NFL player. Rodgers was just 27 years old when he reached that goal. He was at the top of the sports world, but he still wasn't satisfied. "I'd love to go back [to the Super Bowl] at least a few more times," he said.

Rodgers reached the milestone of 300 touchdown passes faster than any other NFL quarterback has. He also did it with fewer passing attempts. He's the only NFL passer to throw 300 touchdowns with fewer than 100 interceptions.

Favre to move on from the team. Others say the time he spent watching Favre was a valuable learning experience for Rodgers. Here's how Rodgers compares to other legends on the NFL's all-time passing touchdowns list:

Player	Career touchdowns
Peyton Manning	539
Brett Favre	508
Drew Brees	471
Tom Brady	464
Dan Marino	420
Fran Tarkenton	342
Eli Manning	324
Philip Rivers	318
Aaron Rodgers	307
Ben Roethlisberger	306

Source Notes

10 "How Playing Multiple Sports as a Kid Helped Aaron Rodgers Become a Better Athlete," *Stack*, last modified January 18, 2017, http://www.stack.com/a /how-playing-multiple-sports-as-a-kid-helped-aaron -rodgers-become-a-better-athlete.

16 Scott David, "Aaron Rodgers Is Structuring His Life Like Tom Brady in Order to Play Football into His 40s," *Business Insider*, September 10, 2017, http:// www.businessinsider.com/aaron-rodgers-tom-brady -diet-workouts-play-nfl-40s-2017-7.

17 Matthew Jussim, "Aaron Rodgers Talks Offseason Training, Yoga, and Eating Habits: 'I Want to Play Another 10 Years,'" *Men's Fitness*, August 7, 2017, http://www.mensfitness.com/sports/football/aaron -rodgers-talks-offseason-training-yoga-and-eating -habits-i-want-play-another-10.

21 Mina Kimes, "The Search for Aaron Rodgers," *ESPN the Magazine*, August 30, 2017, http://www.espn.com /espn/feature/story/_/page/enterpriseRodgers/green -bay-packers-qb-aaron-rodgers-unmasked-searching.

27 Kimes, "The Search."

Glossary

community college: a two-year government-supported school

conference: a group of teams that play against one another

flexible: able to bend easily

interceptions: passes caught by the opposing team that give them possession of the ball

NFL Draft: an event in which NFL teams take turns choosing new players

point guard: a basketball player who handles the ball a lot and passes to other players

Pro Bowl: a game held to honor those chosen as that season's best NFL players

scholarship: money to help pay for school

wide receiver: a football player whose main job is to catch passes

yoga: exercises that help the body and the mind

Braun, Eric. *Tom Brady*. Minneapolis: Lerner Publications, 2017.

Green Bay Packers
http://www.packers.com

Morey, Allan. *The Green Bay Packers Story*. Minneapolis: Bellwether Media, 2017.

NFL Rush
http://www.nflrush.com

Savage, Jeff. *Football Super Stats*. Minneapolis: Lerner Publications, 2018.

Sports Illustrated Kids
https://www.sikids.com

Index

Atlanta Falcons, 5, 7

Butte College, 11

Chico, CA, 8–9

Favre, Brett, 6

Midwest Athletes Against
    Childhood Cancer Fund, 22
Most Valuable Player (MVP), 19,
    24–25

Obama, Barack, 23

Pro Bowl, 24

Rodgers, Ed, 9
Rodgers, Jordan, 20

Super Bowl XLV, 19, 25

University of California, Berkeley
    (Cal), 11–12

yoga, 17

Photo Acknowledgments

Image credits: Jonathan Daniel/Getty Images, p. 2; Todd Kirkland/Icon
Sportswire/Getty Images, pp. 4–5; Brett Davis/USA Today Sports/Newscom,
p. 6; Kevin C. Cox/Getty Images, p. 7; Robert B. Stanton/WireImage/
Getty Images, pp. 8, 11; Focus on Sport/Getty Images, p. 9; Seth Poppel
Yearbook Library, p. 10; Chris Trotman/Getty Images, p. 12; Jeff Gross/
Getty Images, p. 13; Larry Radloff/Icon Sportswire/Getty Images, pp. 14, 17;
Wesley Hitt/Getty Images, p. 16; Ron T. Ennis/Fort Worth Star-Telegram/
MCT/Getty Images, p. 18; Streeter Lecka/Getty Images, p. 19; Liam Goodner/
Shutterstock.com, p. 20; Steve Granitz/WireImage/Getty Images, p. 21;
© Jeff Hanisch/USA TODAY Sports, p. 22; Mark Wilson/Getty Images, p. 23;
Roger L. Wollenberg/UPI/Newscom, p. 24; Allen Fredrickson//REUTERS/
Newscom, p. 25; Rob Tringali/SportsChrome/Getty Images, p. 26.

Cover: Jonathan Daniel/Getty Images.